LEARN TO
sew

LEARN TO
sew

Alison Reid

PHOTOGRAPHS BY
John Heseltine

STERLING

New York / London
www.sterlingpublishing.com

Library of Congress Cataloging-in-Publication
Data Available
10 9 8 7 6 5 4 3 2 1

Published in 2008 by Sterling Publishing Co., Inc
387 Park Avenue South, New York, NY10016
Copyright © Coats Crafts UK
A Coats publication

First published in Great Britain in 2008 by
Coats Crafts UK
Lingfield Point
McMullen Road
Darlington
Co. Durham
DL1 1YJ

Distributed in Canada by Sterling Publishing
c/o Canadian Manda Group, 165 Dufferin Street,
Toronto, Ontario, Canada M6K 3H6

Printed in China

Sterling ISBN 978-1-4027-6334-2

For information about custom editions, special sales,
premium and corporate purchases, please contact
Sterling Special Sales Department at 800-805-5489
or specialsales@sterlingpublishing.com

Editor Katie Hardwicke
Design Anne Wilson
Illustrations Alison Reid
Photography John Heseltine
Styling Susan Berry

Contents

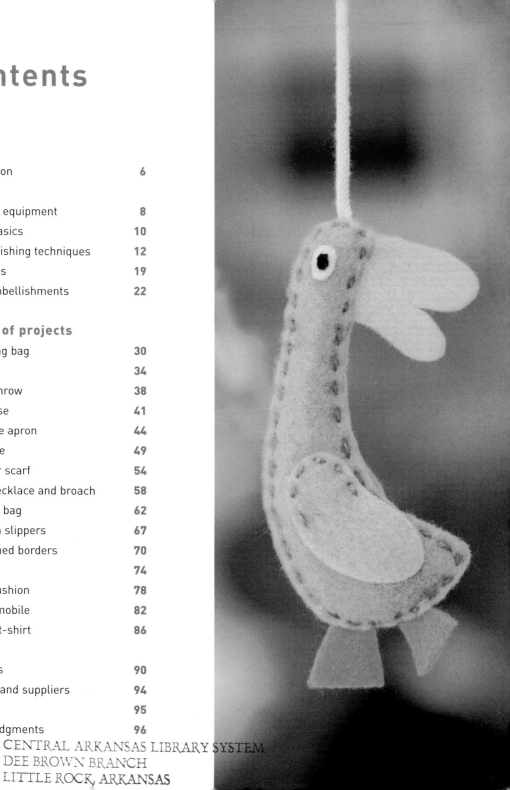

Introduction

Learning how to sew is very rewarding. Not only can you make some great things for your home, you can make things for yourself, your family, and your friends.

This book uses both hand and machine sewing, and some very basic hand embroidery. I am assuming you have a sewing machine, which comes with its own manual showing you how to use it. As each sewing machine differs in how it is threaded and set up, and the different attachments it has for specific purposes, you need to practice working with it until you are comfortable using it, and can stitch with it easily and well. If you find it difficult to get going, ask someone who has used a machine before to show you. If you are thinking of buying a machine, get some advice first. There are many different kinds, and some are more user-friendly than others.

To sew anything with a degree of professional finish, you need to plan your work and set yourself up properly. Organize all the elements you will need first (and keep your basic small items of kit in a little work box). Sew in a good light, at a table, with an ironing board and iron set up close by. It is really important to press each stage of your work as you complete it, and

to take time and trouble when cutting out fabric, taking measurements, and pinning fabrics together.

The first part of the book covers the basics you will need for the projects that follow, while the second part is devoted to a range of different projects, hopefully enticing you to make some of them!

I teach students at an art college, many of whom have never sewn anything in their lives until they get to the class, and I have used this experience in creating the ideas in this book, making them achievable for people of every skill level. However, some more advanced sewing techniques, such as making and altering clothing to fit, are not covered, as this requires another skill level to produce wearable results. Some projects are easy and straightforward, and are marked with a single star. Intermediate ones are marked with a double star, and more challenging ones with three stars.

The materials in this book are all Coats haberdashery products or Rowan fabrics. You can check out the website and addresses at the back of the book.

I hope you enjoy making the items in this book as much as I have enjoyed designing and making them myself.

Tools and equipment

The following is a list of basic tools and equipment you will need to make the projects in this book, and for any other hand or machine sewing you might undertake. Keep the small pieces of equipment in a work box.

Sewing machine

You will need a sewing machine to make the most of the projects in this book. Please refer to your individual sewing machine manual for the instructions relating to stitch settings, tensions, and needle sizes, etc.

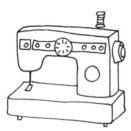

Iron

An iron is an integral part in the finishing process of all the sewing projects. There is a golden rule to keep in mind to achieve a professional finish: whenever you complete a stage in the making up of a project, press that finished stage.

Sewing thread

There are different thicknesses and different types of thread. The projects in this book are made up using the following types of thread: **Stranded embroidery cotton** is used for decorative hand stitching, as is the thicker **tapestry wool** (made from pure wool). **Cotton sewing thread** is used for machine sewing cotton fabrics.

Hand-sewing needles

There are various types and sizes of hand-sewing needles. For every project in this book that requires hand sewing, the needle recommended for use will be listed in the section entitled: "You will need."

Fabric-marking pencil

Used for marking out patterns/motifs on your fabric before cutting. It is designed so that it can be washed or brushed off on completion of the project.

Dressmaker's pins

Dressmaker's pins are required for temporarily securing seams, motifs, or embellishments before sewing.

Dressmaker's shears

A good sharp pair of heavy-duty scissors or shears are essential for cutting out long lengths of fabric.

Embroidery scissors

A small, sharp pair of scissors are extremely useful for cutting stray ends of thread as well as cutting more intricate details into fabric.

Tape measure

Useful when the need to make precision measurements arises.

Iron-on adhesives

Conventional interfacing fabric has adhesive on one side. Iron-on adhesive paper comes in sheet form, with dry glue on one side of a piece of tracing paper. The tracing paper can be drawn on in pencil so the design can be marked out. After cutting out your motif, the glue side of the tracing paper is placed down on the wrong side of the fabric, and a hot iron is run over the top of the tracing paper, which is peeled off to reveal the newly glued fabric. The motif is then placed glue-side down on top of the right side of another piece of fabric. The iron is then applied again to the motif so that it bonds with the other piece of fabric.

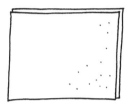

Loop turner

This gadget is used for turning narrow stitched tubes to the right side out. There is a hook and a latch at one end of the turner to enable the easy turning of the tube.

Revolving punch pliers

These are ideal when you require a small perfect circle to be cut in fabric. The pliers have a variety of different-sized circles to choose from: revolve the pliers to choose the appropriate size.

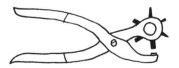

Sewing basics

The following guidelines explain simple rules or techniques that will help in any general sewing project.

Fabric

The tightly woven edges on the sides of a length of fabric are called the selvedges. The threads that run parallel to the selvedge are called the warp threads, while the threads that run across from selvedge to selvedge are called the weft threads.

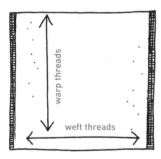

common fabric terms

Some of the illustrations in this book will be marked with the abbreviations RS and WS. This makes reference to which way up the fabric needs to be placed. RS = right side and WS = wrong side.

Grain lines

The straight grain of a fabric runs parallel to the warp threads. This is the most common way of laying out a paper pattern onto fabric. The bias runs at a 45-degree angle across the straight grain. Cutting fabric in this way gives stretch to the material. It can then adapt itself to any shape when sewn.

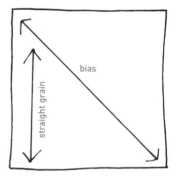

fabric grain

Cutting out

When cutting out fabric, it is best to lay it out on a non-slip surface. Make sure when using pattern pieces that you pin the pattern pieces to the chosen fabric carefully. Always use sharp scissors when cutting out the fabric.

sharp scissors for cutting fabric

Machine stitching

Please refer to your sewing machine manual for instructions relating to stitch settings and tension. Generally a straight stitch should be set at a length of 2.5. To secure any lines of stitching (back baste), run a few stitches forward and then run a few stitches in reverse stitching (refer to your manual) before stitching the complete line. Just before you reach the end of the line of stitching, repeat this step by running a few stitches backward and finish off running a few stitches forward to the end of the line.

Seams

Almost every project in this book will require plain seams when making up. Make sure that the fabric is cut out as neatly as possible. A seam is made by placing two pieces of fabric right sides together. Pin the two pieces together to stop any movement while sewing. Then sew a straight line of stitching 1/2in (1cm) in from the raw edges of the fabric. You can remove the pins easily as you sew. Keep to the suggested seam allowance and press the seams open as you complete each seam.

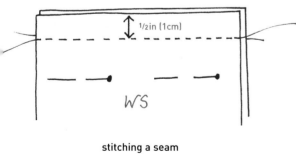

stitching a seam

Securing edges

To stop fabric fraying, set the sewing machine to zigzag stitch and turn the raw edges to the wrong side and stitch in place before sewing the seams.

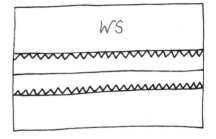

zigzag stitch

If you have access to an overlocking machine, you can finish off the edges following the guidelines in the overlocker manual. A less durable finish is made using pinking shears to finish the raw edges.

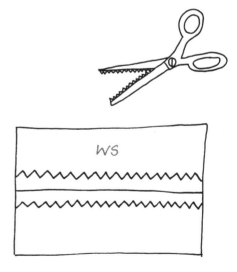

raw edges secured with pinking shears

Useful finishing techniques

The following techniques are used in some of the projects in this book, and are useful for other general sewing projects, too.

Rouleau tubes
These can be used as button loops or as a decorative device – for example, looped to form a horseshoe shape when inserted into a seam. They are cut on the bias of the fabric—in other words at an angle of 45 degrees to the straight grain—as this allows the fabric to curve easily without folds. You will need a loop turner to turn the fabric inside out once stitched.

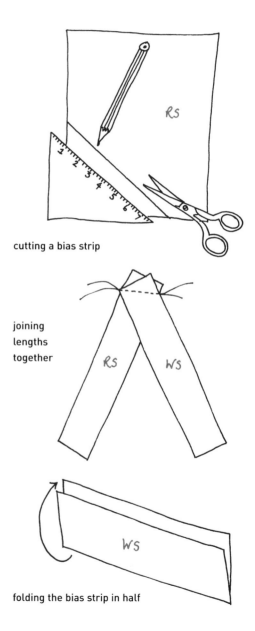

cutting a bias strip

joining
lengths
together

folding the bias strip in half

1 Cut a bias strip from your chosen fabric, using a set-square to achieve the correct 45 degree angle. If you need to join long lengths together, then place the cut strips together and sew at the angle shown. With right sides together, fold the fabric in half lengthwise.

2 Set the sewing machine to a small stitch (such as 2), and as you stitch hold both ends of the fabric taut, so the fabric is stretched as it is stitched. Make sure to back baste (see page 11) at the beginning and at the end of the tubing to secure it.

3 Once stitched, cut back any excess fabric from the seam, taking care not to cut through the stitches. This is essential if your tubing is very narrow.

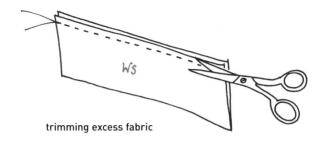

trimming excess fabric

4 Put a loop turner up through the inside of the tubing and hook the latch part carefully onto the top end of the tube.

5 Very gently ease the tubing through itself, until all of the tube is right side out. Take care not to pull the tubing too hard as the stitches could split. The tubing can hen be cut to the required length.

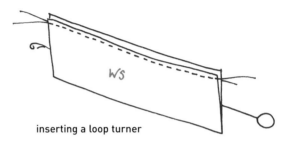

inserting a loop turner

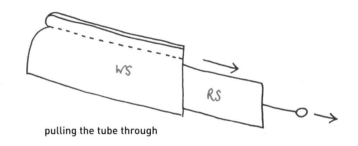

pulling the tube through

Button loops
Rouleau loops can be used as a fastening. By inserting the rouleau loop into a seam or by sewing it to the reverse of a piece of fabric, it can be used as a loop to fasten a button closing. To make a buttonhole, follow the instructions in your sewing machine manual.

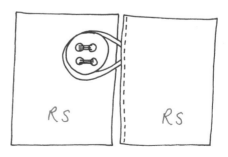

sewing the rouleau loop into the seam opposite the button

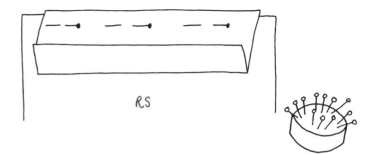

pinning the bias binding to the edge of the fabric

RS

Bias binding

Bias binding is useful for enclosing raw fabric edges to prevent fraying on a hem or a seam, for example.

1 Place the bias binding (opened out) along the raw edge of the fabric, right sides together. Pin along the first crease line of the binding. Make sure that the raw edges of the fabric and the binding always meet.

2 Now sew along the crease line, removing the pins as you go.

3 Turn the fabric so the wrong side is facing you. Fold the binding over the raw edge and pin into place, with the folded edge of the binding just above the row of stitches.

4 Turn the fabric to the right side and stitch almost at the edge of the binding.

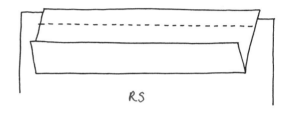

RS

stitching the bias binding in place

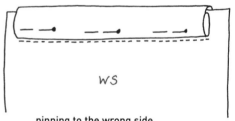

WS

pinning to the wrong side

stitching along the edge of the binding

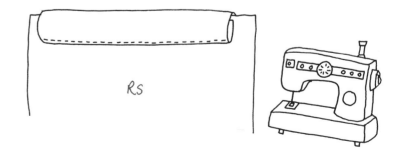

RS

Special edging shapes

You can create shapes to use as edging details, such as scallops or tabs.

1 Decide on the shape and mark it out on a piece of card. (For the scalloped edge on the pillowcase on page 49, a compass was used to ensure precision.) Don't forget to add a seam allowance of 1/2in (1cm) at the bottom edge and also along the edge where the shape is to be inserted.

2 Cut out the card template (see page 18) and position it on two layers of fabric held in place with pins. Make sure that the template follows the straight grain of the fabric. Using a fabric-marking pencil, draw carefully around your template, moving and repositioning it if a repeating pattern is required.

3 Set your sewing machine to straight stitch, setting 2. Stitch all the way around the shape. At the curved edges, stop the sewing machine and raise the presser foot to reposition the fabric, keeping the needle down; doing this gradually around the curve ensures an even, neat curve.

4 When you have finished stitching, cut into any corners and curves as shown, taking care not to cut the stitches themselves.

5 Turn the shapes the right side out and gently push out any corners or curves with the eraser end of a pencil. Finish off by pressing with a steam iron.

drawing around the shape onto card, adding a seam allowance all around

place the template on the fabric

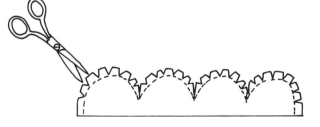

cutting the curved edges to ease the seam

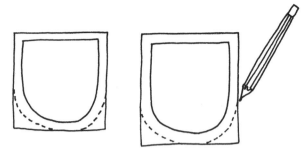

making the paper pattern

Patch pockets

1 First, decide how big your patch pocket is to be. (If the pocket is functional, make it big enough for your hand to fit into.) The dimensions for the apron pockets on page 45 are intended to be functional, they are 9 x 8in (22 x 19cm) and 7 x 8in (18 x 19cm)—two different sizes are used to allow for a fabric detail on the finished pocket.

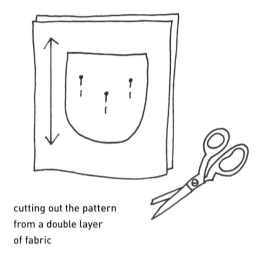

cutting out the pattern
from a double layer
of fabric

2 Draw out the pocket shape onto a piece of paper first and gently round off the two bottom corners. Cut out the pattern pieces remembering to add a 1/2in (1cm) seam allowance all the way round.

3 Place the large pattern onto one selection of fabric and the smaller pattern onto the other—you can cut two at a time by folding your fabric in half. Pin your fabric into place and cut out the pocket shapes.

4 Now take a large pocket and a small pocket and place right sides together, pinning in place (as shown left). Sew a 1/2in (1cm) seam along the top of the pocket and then press open the seam.

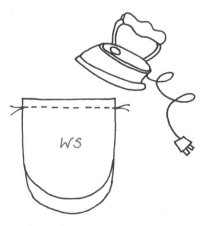

WS

sewing a large and small pocket together

5 With right sides still together, maneuver the fabric so that the curves meet up. Again, sew a 1/2in (1cm) seam allowance all the way around except for an opening on the side of about 2in (5cm). You will need this to be able to turn the pocket the right sides out. Before you do this, cut into the corners as shown below to allow ease. Make sure that you do not cut into your stitches.

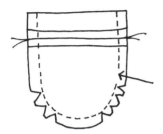

cutting into the curve to ease the seam

6 Turn the pocket right sides out. Press to ensure all seams are neat and lying flat, including the opening; this will be secured by top stitching. Position your pocket on your garment shape and pin into place. Top stitch, using a straight stitch all of the way around apart from the top opening, to firmly attach the pocket to your garment.

As an extra feature, and for added strength, you can sew a detail as shown in the diagram below right, or set your sewing machine to satin stitch and sew the top edges of your pocket (below left).

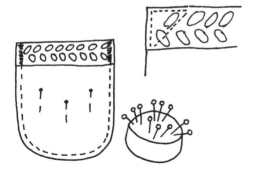

pinning the pocket in place
and top stitching to secure

Making a template

Some of the projects require you to make a card template of a motif or shape to create a matching fabric shape.

1 Get together tracing paper, thin card or pattern paper, a soft lead pencil, a fabric-marking pencil, some pins, and a pair of sharp scissors.

2 Trace over the edges of the design onto tracing paper using a pencil. Enlarge your motif on a photocopier to the required size if necessary, then trace.

3 Turn the tracing paper over and scribble over the outline in pencil on the reverse side of the paper.

4 Place the tracing paper, reverse side down, on the card or pattern paper for the template and draw over the outline again, which will transfer your penciled outline.

5 Cut out the transferred shape from the card and position this on your chosen fabric, securing with pins if necessary.

6 Draw around the card template with a fabric-marking pencil, remove the template, and cut out the fabric shape with small sharp scissors.

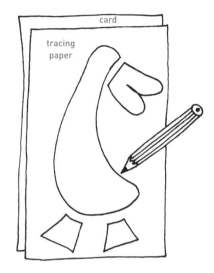

drawing over the outline to transfer the design

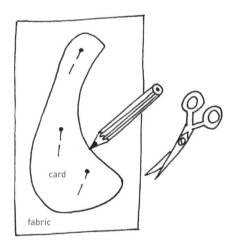

drawing around the card template before cutting out the shape

Fastenings

These are some basic fastening devices for your projects. Button loops are easier than buttonholes, which are not as easy for first-time stitchers. Refer to the techniques for rouleau loops (see page 12) for providing the fastening for your buttons.

Sewing on a button

1 Position the button on your fabric where required, matching up with the corresponding buttonhole if necessary.

2 Thread your needle and tie a knot in the end. Take the needle up from the back of the fabric to the front, making sure that you are taking the needle through one of the holes on the button.

3 Bring the needle back down through a second hole on the button from the top down through the fabric. Pull the thread through but leave a little bit of slack, so that the button is not sitting tightly on the surface of the fabric.

4 Continue until there are enough stitches to secure the button. If your button has four holes then work them in the same way.

5 Take the needle in between where the top of the fabric meets the button. Wind the cotton around the shank of threads you have created to give added strength to the stitches. Finish off by taking the needle through to the back and sew a few stitches.

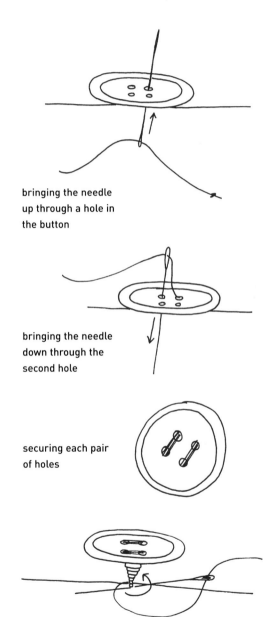

bringing the needle up through a hole in the button

bringing the needle down through the second hole

securing each pair of holes

winding the cotton around the shank of threads

Self-cover buttons

1 Place the template onto the wrong side of your chosen fabric and draw around the circle. Cut out.

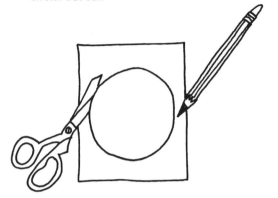

cutting out the circle from fabric

2 Thread your hand-sewing needle and tie a knot in the end. Sew small running stitches (see page 22) around the edge of the circle but not too close to it. Leave the ends of thread and needle attached.

sewing running stitch around the edge

3 Place the front section of the button face down onto the wrong side of the fabric circle. Making sure the button is central, gently draw and gather up the stitches, so that the button becomes covered with fabric.

gathering the fabric around the button

4 Take the needle and the ends of thread and sew a few stitches to secure the gathers. Cut off the waste thread.

securing the gathers with a few stitches

5 Now take the back piece of the button and press down into the main body of the button. Your button is now ready to sew into place.

pressing the back piece onto the button

Zippers

It is quickest and easiest to put a zipper in using a sewing machine with a zipper foot attachment. Stitch just outside the metal teeth of the zipper.

INSERTING A ZIPPER

1 When inserting a zipper it is easier to insert into an area to be seamed. First, fold over by 1/2in (1cm) the two edges of the fabric where the zipper is to be inserted, and press them.

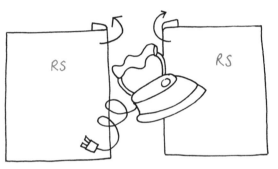

folding and pressing the fabric

2 Fasten up the zipper and lay facing upward on a flat surface. Now lay the pressed edge of one piece of fabric alongside the teeth on one side of the zipper. Repeat on the other side. Pin in place. Fold the ends of the zipper tape under. If you replace the pins with hand-sewn basting stitches it will be easier when machine sewing the zipper.

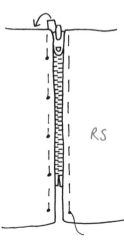

pinning zipper in place

3 Attach the zipper foot to your sewing machine (refer to your sewing machine manual for guidance). Open up the zipper and position the machine foot at the top of the zipper on the left hand side. Using straight stitch, sew down the length of the zipper close to the teeth until you reach the zipper. Leave the needle down in your fabric.

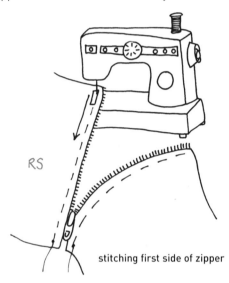

stitching first side of zipper

4 Lift up the zipper foot and fasten the zipper. Pivot the fabric and sew across the bottom of the zipper. Again leave the needle down in the fabric and, with the zipper still fastened, pivot your fabric and sew up the other side of the zipper. Remove the basting stitches from your fabric.

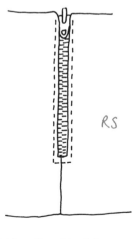

stitching other side of zipper

21

Fabric embellishments

Here are a few basic embellishments that you can apply to your fabrics or projects, including hand embroidery stitches, quilting (in which you sandwich layers of fabric together), and appliqué (in which you apply one fabric to another as decoration).

Running stitch

This is an attractive, graphic linear stitch.

1 Mark out the area you are going to stitch. Take your hand-sewing needle, thread it and tie a knot in the end of the thread.

2 Bring the needle up from the back of the fabric to the front and then pick up small areas of fabric on the needle as shown. The stitches should be of equal length and distance apart. Pull the needle through.

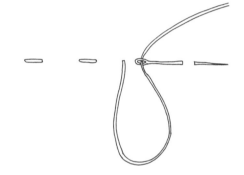

evenly-spaced running stitch

Satin stitch

This is a filling stitch, used to cover a design with stitches.

1 Mark out the area you are going to stitch with a fabric-marking pencil.

2 Bring the needle up from the back of the fabric through to the front at one end of your chosen embroidery design. Take the thread across the fabric and insert the needle again at the opposite side of the design, and repeat to create long, flat stitches, closely and evenly worked together, across your fabric.

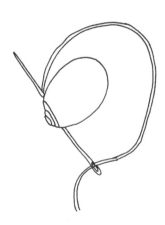

closely-worked satin stitch

Blanket stitch

This is a decorative stitch used on the edge of a fabric or it can be used to stitch two edges of fabric together. It generally uses a thicker embroidery thread or tapestry yarn and a chenille sewing needle.

1 Hold the edge to be worked on away from you with the right side of the fabric facing you. Bring the threaded needle, with a knot in the thread to prevent slippage, from the back of the fabric through to the front about 1/4in (5mm) from the edge.

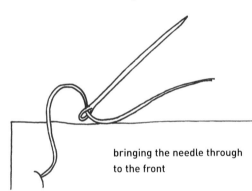

bringing the needle through
to the front

2 Then take the needle to the back of the fabric again, looping over the edge of the fabric at this point. Bring the needle up through the back of the fabric about 1/4in (5mm) from the previous stitch. Loop the thread over and under the needle and pull the needle all of the way through the fabric.

looping the thread over the
edge and bringing the
needle back to the front

3 Repeat these steps around the edge of your fabric, leaving 1/4in (5mm) between stitches and keeping 1/4in (5mm) from the edge of the fabric.

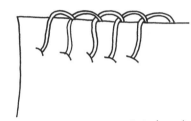

repeating at 1/4in (5mm) intervals

Buttonhole stitch

If you want to make a hand-worked buttonhole, cut an appropriately sized slit and use buttonhole stitch to finish the edges. This is a closely worked form of blanket stitch: butt the stitches up close together rather than leaving a gap as with blanket stitch.

French knot

This makes decorative little bobbles on the surface of the fabric.

1 Take your needle from the back of the fabric to the front at the point at which you want to create your French knot. Make a small running stitch, but leave the needle in the fabric.

making a small running stitch

2 While holding the fabric and the needle in one hand, use the other hand to wrap the thread several times around the needle—the more wraps you complete the bigger the French knot will be.

wrapping the thread around the needle

3 Draw the needle through the wraps of thread while keeping your thumb on the threads to prevent them from tangling. As close to the French knot as possible, take your needle through to the back of the fabric.

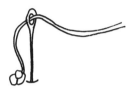

taking the needle through to the back

4 Secure the French knot with a couple of stitches at the back.

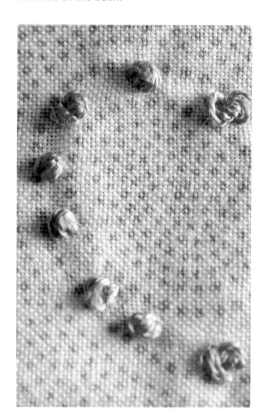

Quilting

This is a way of joining two fabrics together with decorative surface stitching, using batting to pad the layers. There are many varying weights of batting available. The thickness you choose depends on the project.

1 First, cut out two identical sized pieces of fabric, one for the front and the other for the back. Then cut out a piece of batting to match. Use a template if necessary.

2 Sandwich the batting in between the two pieces of fabric.

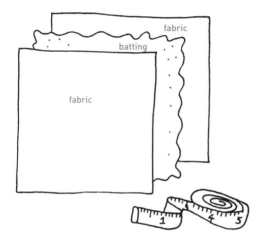

sandwiching the batting between the fabric

3 Secure the layers together with pins. Using a hand-sewing needle and thread, stitch large basting stitches across the fabric sandwich at 45 degree angles. Repeat until the fabric is covered.

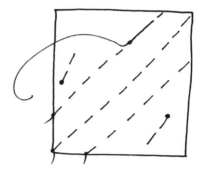

basting stitches at 45 degree angle

4 Repeat this step, working in the opposite direction, leaving spaces of equal distance between the stitching lines. Your fabric is now ready for quilting by machine in your chosen pattern.

fabric prepared for machine quilting

5 After quilting your fabric on the sewing machine, carefully remove the basting stitches from all the layers.

Appliqué shapes with adhesive

Using iron-on adhesive paper allows you to cut out shapes in fabric and iron them onto the main fabric in any chosen position. If you are using several different fabrics, or there are different components to your design, treat each one as a separate item.

1 Draw your design on paper, and mark each pattern piece with (RS) for right side.

drawing the design

2 Cut out the paper pattern pieces.

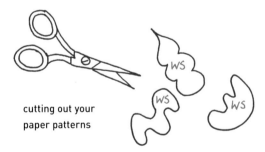

cutting out your paper patterns

3 Place your pattern pieces with the right side (RS) facing down onto the paper side of the adhesive paper. (This is important to do otherwise you will create a reverse of your image.) Draw around each shape, and then roughly cut them out from the paper.

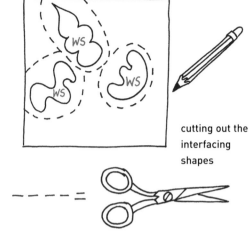

cutting out the interfacing shapes

4 Place each piece down on the wrong side of the selected fabric, making sure that the glue side of the adhesive paper is facing down and the paper side is facing up. Put a piece of scrap fabric over the top of the pieces to ensure the glue does not melt onto the sole plate of the iron. Using a hot iron, press the fabrics for about two seconds.

5 When the fabric has cooled, cut out the shapes required and remove the paper.

6 Position your cut out fabrics on the right side of your project fabric and, using the scrap fabric to protect the design, press again. Check that the shapes have bonded properly, if not then press again.

bonding the fabric shapes to the main fabric

Pom-poms

To make pom-poms you will need either a piece of card and a compass or a pom-pom making kit. The bigger the pom-pom templates, the bigger the pom-pom!

1 Cut two circular cardboard templates with a small circular opening at both of their centers.

cutting two template disks

2 Place the two disks together and wind your wool tightly and closely around the templates by going over the outside edge and up through the center.

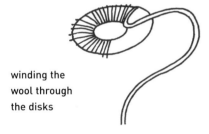

winding the wool through the disks

3 As the hole in the center begins to get smaller you can thread the yarn through a large darning needle, making it easier to handle. Continue with this process until the hole in the center disappears. Using very

cutting through the wool between the two disks

sharp scissors, cut around the outside edge between the two cardboard templates.

4 Take some strong thread in a matching color and pass it between the templates. Pull and tie firmly in a double knot.

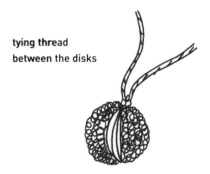

tying thread between the disks

5 Carefully remove the templates. Fluff out the pom-pom and trim any excess ends.

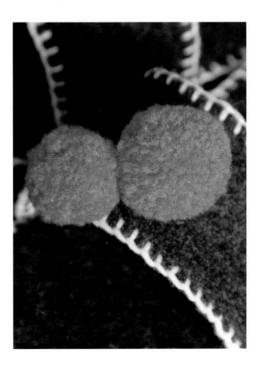

gallery of projects

simple things to sew for the home, for yourself, and for your kids

Drawstring bag

✪✪ *This little drawstring bag measures approximately 9¹/₂ x 12¹/₂in (24 x 32cm). Hang it on a closet door and use it as bathroom or bedroom tidy, or make a larger one for a laundry bag.*

You will need
¹/₂yd (0.5m) striped cotton fabric for bag and ¹/₂yd (0.5m) matching plain cotton fabric for trim
Compass
Fabric-marking pencil
Chenille needle
Stranded embroidery cotton in two colors
Revolving punch pliers
Sewing thread to match
Safety pin
Cord

Preparing the fabric

1 On the straight grain of the main fabric for the bag, cut out two pieces of fabric measuring 20 x 14$\frac{1}{2}$in (50 x 37cm), one for the outer bag and one for the lining.

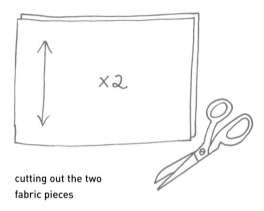

cutting out the two
fabric pieces

2 Next, prepare your trim. Cut a 20in (50cm) length of fabric. With a fabric-marking pencil, mark out semicircles along the fabric, using a compass set to 1$\frac{3}{4}$in (4cm). Cut out the semicircles to create a scalloped edge. Using stranded embroidery cotton, decorate the trim with running stitch and then use the revolving punch pliers to add further decoration (see page 33).

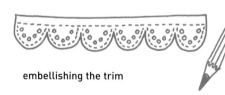

embellishing the trim

Making the drawstring bag

3 Pin the trim across the 20-in (50-cm) width of the right side of the pre-cut fabric, about one third of the way up. Using straight stitch, sew the trim to the fabric.

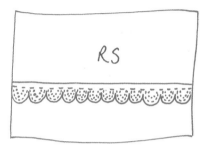

sewing the trim to the fabric

4 With the right sides together, fold the decorated fabric piece over, making sure that the trim aligns. Secure with pins and, using a $\frac{1}{2}$in (1cm) seam allowance, machine stitch across the bottom and up the side. When sewing the long side leave the last 2$\frac{1}{4}$in (6cm) open. Repeat with the other piece of fabric for the lining, stitching all of the long side. Press all the seams open. Turn right sides out.

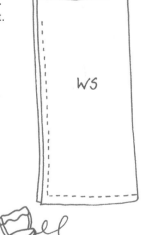

sewing the
seams, right
sides together

5 Top stitch the 2¹⁄₄in (6cm) opening on both sides and press.

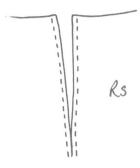

top stitching both sides of the opening

6 With wrong sides together, place the lining inside the outer part of the bag. Push down into the corners to ensure a neat fit.

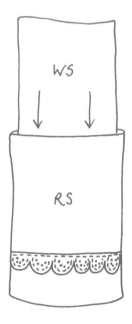

putting the lining inside the bag,
wrong sides together

7 Fold the top of the outer section of the bag over by 1³⁄₄in (4cm) toward the lining and do the same with the lining, folding it toward the outer section.

folding over the top of the bag to form a channel

8 Pin into place and top stitch all around the top edge. Do the same again 1in (2.5cm) below to form the channel for the cord. To finish off you can use a satin stitch to strengthen the opening (see page 22).

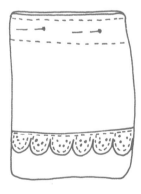

stitching the channel

9 Attach a safety pin to one end of the cord and feed it through the opening of the channel, pushing it all the way around until it comes out through the opening at the other end. Tie the two ends of cord together in a knot to secure.

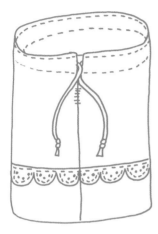

feeding the cord through the channel

pulling the cord together to finish the bag

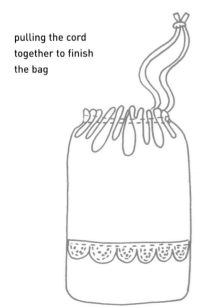

Tea cozy

✪✪✪ *Tea parties are a lovely way to socialize and, when you do, you need a cozy to keep your teapot warm. This one is quilted with batting, making it very effective. The shapes around the edge give a fun, modern feel.*

You will need
Pattern paper
Teapot
1/2yd (0.5m) spotted cotton fabric and 1/2yd (0.5m) plain cotton fabric
Fabric-marking pencil
Batting
Sewing thread to match
Bias binding maker (optional) or bias binding to match

Making a template
1 Lay a large piece of pattern paper out on a flat surface. Carefully lay your teapot down on its side on the pattern paper. Draw a semicircle that extends beyond your teapot by 2in (5cm). Include the spout, handle, and

lid. Draw a straight line across the base, adding 1¹/2in (4cm) below.

2 Cut out the paper pattern as a template for both the fabric and batting.

Quilting the tea cozy
3 Prepare your batting and fabric for quilting (see page 25), cutting on the straight grain. If your sewing machine has a quilting guide, attach it to your machine to help control the stitching. Have a look at the decorative

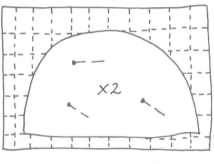

pinning the pattern to the quilted fabric

stitches your machine can create, such as the scallop stitch used here. Quilt the fabric. Pin your pattern to the quilted fabric and cut out two shapes.

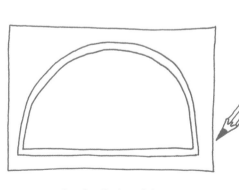

drawing the template

EDGING SHAPE TEMPLATES

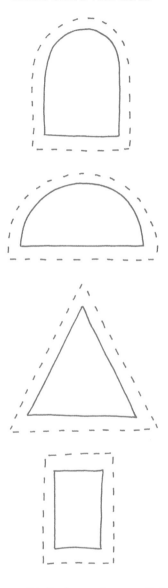

- - - - ¹/₂in (1cm) seam allowance added around shapes

enlarge the templates by 75% and cut two pieces of fabric for each shape

Inserting the fabric shapes

4 Make templates from the shapes shown on the left and prepare the fabric shapes for the edge of the cozy (see page 15). Work each shape individually.

5 Next, take one quilted semicircle. With the right sides facing, place the prepared shapes around the outside of the semicircle, facing inward. Carefully lay the other quilted semicircle on top so that right sides are facing and pin around the outside edge to hold the shapes in place. Using a 1/2in (1cm) seam allowance, stitch around the semicircle.

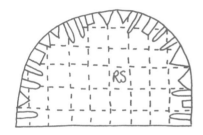

inserting the fabric shapes between the quilted fabric semicircles

6 Cut into the seam to allow ease when turning back. Remove the pins and turn the right way out.

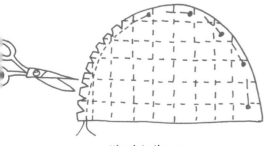

cutting into the seam

7 Using bias binding (prepared from your chosen fabric or already prepared, see page 14), stitch in place around the bottom of your tea cozy to finish off the raw edge.

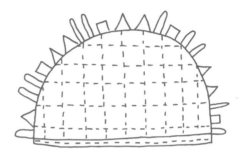

adding bias binding to the bottom edge

Fringed throw

✪✪ *This simple throw, measuring 64¹/₂ x 43¹/₄in (164 x 110cm), is simple to make, but you could easily add some appliqué motifs (see page 26) before making it up. The fringe is made in sections to whatever width you prefer.*

You will need
2yd (2m) plain cotton fabric
Card
Tapestry wool yarn in contrasting color
Tissue paper
Sewing thread to match
Hand-sewing needle

Preparing the fabric
1 Cut out two pieces of fabric measuring 65 x 44in (166 x 112cm), including seam allowances all the way around.

Making the fringing
2 Cut a length of card to a width of at least 3in (8cm) —it can be any length but the longer the better. Cut out the middle section of the card, leaving a space wide enough to allow your machine presser foot to pass down it. Cut small slots at the ends of the card to hold the yarn (see below left).

3 Wrap the yarn around the card using the slots to secure the ends. The more closely wound the wool, the thicker the fringe will be (but remember that you need to sew over it, so don't make it too thick).

4 Place a strip of tissue paper over the area to be stitched to prevent the wool from tangling in the presser foot. You will tear the paper off after sewing. Machine stitch down the center of the card using matching thread. Using a sharp pair of scissors, cut down the sides of the wool.

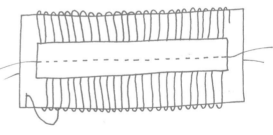

machine stitching down the center of the card, over the tissue paper covering the wool threads

stitching across the threads, with paper removed and threads cut

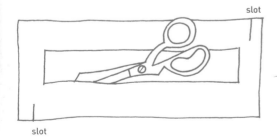

slot

slot

cutting the card to hold the fringing

Making the throw

5 Taking care not to let the fringe tangle, lay it at the end of one piece of fabric for the throw, with right sides facing. The stitching line on the fringe should be inside the fabric. Make sure you have made enough fringing to cover the width at each of the two ends of the throw.

6 Place the remaining piece of fabric carefully on top, right sides facing, and pin into place at frequent intervals to secure the fringe. Sew a 1/2in (1cm) seam allowance all the way around, leaving 4in (10cm) along the top, so that you can turn the throw right sides out through this gap.

7 Turn the throw right sides out, press the opening flat and close with a neat row of hand stitches.

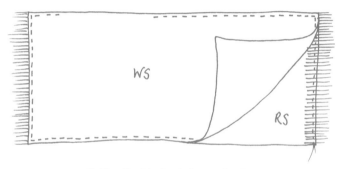

stitching the fringing between the throw

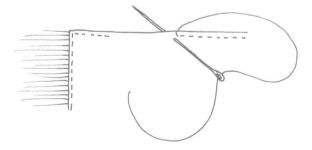

hand stitching the gap closed

Pencil case

✪✪ *This makes a neat pencil case but you could also use it for cosmetics. It measures 9 x 4in (22 x 10cm). The decoration is very simple: just a few buttons but you could also add a row of French knots (see page 24) for variety.*

You will need
1/4yd (0.25m) spotted cotton fabric for the case; scraps of contrasting cotton fabrics for the buttons
Iron-on interfacing
Self-cover buttons: 2 x 3/8in (11mm),
2 x 3/4in (19mm)
Fabric-marking pencil
Zipper: 7in (18cm)
Sewing thread to match
Hand-sewing needle

Preparing the fabric
1 Cut out four pieces of fabric on the straight grain, and two pieces of iron-on interfacing, measuring 9 1/2 x 5 1/2in (24 x 14cm). Sandwich one interfacing sheet between two pieces of fabric, wrong sides together (see page 9).

2 Embellish one of the remaining pieces of fabric. Cover the self-cover buttons with contrasting solid-colored and patterned fabrics (see page 20) and sew on to the front. Bond the wrong sides of the embellished fabric pieces with the remaining interfacing.

3 Fold over 1/2in (1cm) on the long sides of each piece to the wrong side. Pin and press.

bonding the interfacing

pinning the seam allowance

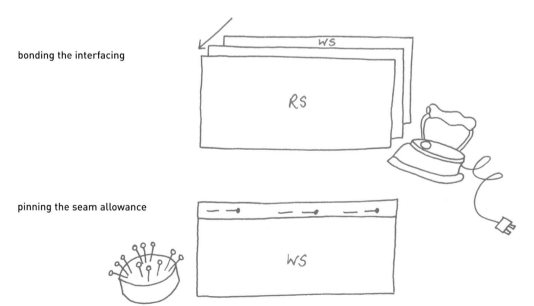

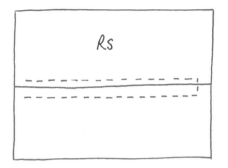

machine stitching the zipper in place

Inserting the zipper

4 To insert the zipper, place the zipper right side up on a flat surface and place the two pieces of fabric right sides up on top, with the folded edges meeting and running down the center of the zipper. Make sure that the zipper is placed centrally. Pin to secure and machine stitch in place (see page 21).

5 Open up the zipper and turn the pencil case inside out so that the right sides are together on the inside. Pin in place. Sew down the two sides and across the bottom with a ½in (1cm) seam allowance. Trim the corners to ease the seam, remove the pins, and turn the pencil case right sides out.

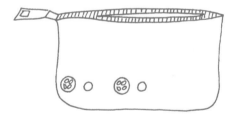

trimming the corners of the stitched seams

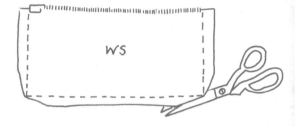

turning the finished pencil case right sides out

Adjustable apron

✪✪✪ *This apron has a pretty retro feel to it. It is lined with a contrasting fabric, which makes a smart edging to the base. You can adjust it to make a longer apron by unbuttoning the tabs. It measures 24¹/₂ x 24¹/₂in (62 x 62cm). Small finishing touches, such as the pocket, waistband edgings, and ties, in the contrast fabric give it a great professional finish.*

You will need
1yd (1m) plain cotton fabric and ¹/₂yd (0.5m) printed cotton fabric to match
Fabric-marking pencil
Sewing thread to match
4 x ¹/₂in (15mm) linen buttons

Preparing the pockets and tabs
1 First prepare two patch pockets in readiness to sew onto your apron front (see page 16). You will need two sizes of fabric, one for the main fabric, and a slightly longer one for the patterned lining, for each pocket, as the lining makes a contrast edging at the top of the pocket. Cut two pieces of main fabric 7 x 8in (18 x 19cm) and two pieces

preparing two patch pockets

of patterned fabric 9 x 8in (22 x 19cm). You will also need to cut out and prepare three tabs (see page 15), each ³/₄ x 2¹/₄in (2 x 6cm),each with a buttonhole or button loop (see page 13).

Making the main part of the apron
2 Cut out on the straight grain a piece of both main and lining fabric, each measuring 25 x 25in (64 x 64cm).

3 On the right side of the main fabric, place the two prepared patch pockets where required, pin and top stitch (see page 17).

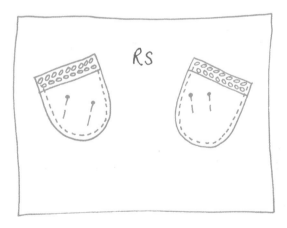

placing the patch pockets

4 Place the two apron sections right sides together and pin. Now position the tabs, raw edge to raw edge, one at the center and the remaining two at least 1¹/₄in (3cm) from the

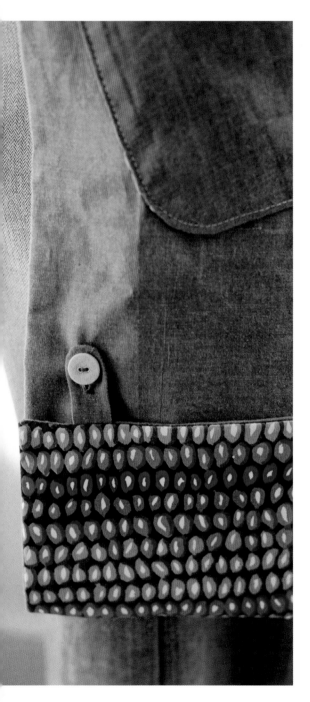

outside edges. Make sure that they are facing inward and upward, toward the main body of the apron.

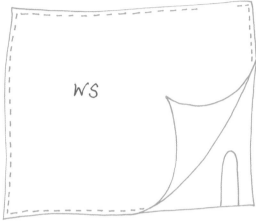

positioning the tabs

5 Using a ¹/₂in (1cm) seam allowance, straight stitch around the rectangle at the two sides and the bottom. Sew along the top but leave an opening of at least 4in (10cm) so that you can turn the apron right sides out. Press open the seams and trim the corners.

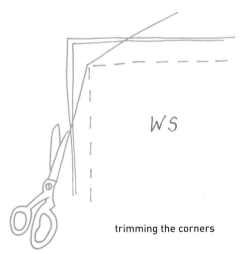

trimming the corners

6 Turn the fabric to the right side through the small opening and press again, ensuring that the seam line is where the fabric folds. Fold over the ¹/₂in (1cm) seams at the opening and press flat.

sewing two parallel lines of stitching along top of apron

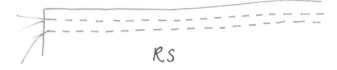

RS

7 Set your sewing machine to a long straight stitch and sew two parallel lines of stitching across the top of the apron. Very carefully gather up your stitching, just enough to give the apron a gentle shape. When you are satisfied with the amount of gathering, set your sewing machine to a standard stitch length of 2.5 and straight stitch across the top of the apron, securing the gathering.

Making the waistband
8 Cut two pieces of both fabrics measuring 36 x 2¹/₄in (88 x 6cm). Place right sides together and pin. Sew the two sides and the top. Press open the seams and cut the corners back. Turn right side out and press.

9 With the solid-colored side facing you, carefully press under the raw edges. Take the solid-colored edge under a little more to reveal a small narrow strip of the patterned fabric underneath. This will give you a decorative edge along the waistband.

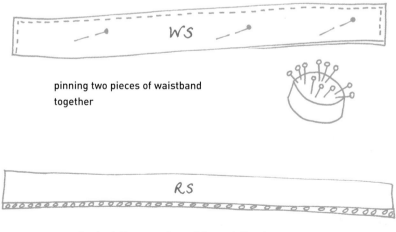

WS

pinning two pieces of waistband together

RS

pressing back the raw edges of the waistband

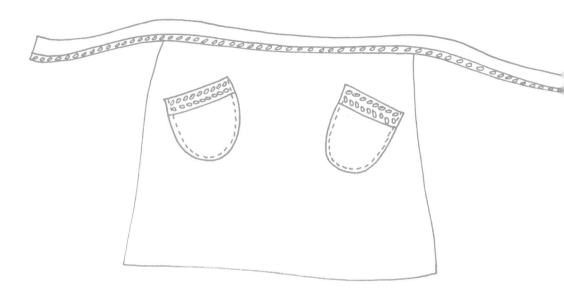

stitching the waistband in place

Finishing the apron

10 Match the center front point for the waistband and apron, and pin into place. Top stitch the waistband to the apron along the unstitched length of the waistband.

11 Fold up the bottom edge of the apron by 4³/₄in (12cm) to reveal the fabric chosen for the back. Line up the buttons with the tabs and stitch in place (see page 19).

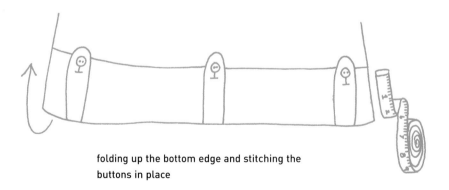

folding up the bottom edge and stitching the buttons in place

Pillowcase

✪✪✪ *This is a simple rectangular pillowcase, measuring 26¼ x 20½in (67 x 52cm) with tape ties and a pretty scalloped border, which you can make in a complementary fabric.*

You will need
Compass
Template card
1yd (1m) pastel patterned cotton fabric and
½yd (0.5m) pastel plain cotton fabric for contrast border
Fabric-marking pencil
Sewing thread to match
Cotton tape

Preparing the scalloped border
1 For the scalloped border you will need to construct your pattern from semicircles. Set your compass to 1in (2.5cm) and draw a 2in (5cm) circle on card. Cut the circle equally in half and use one half as a template for the scallops.

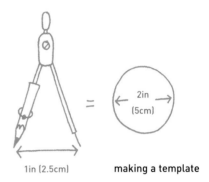

1in (2.5cm)   2in (5cm)

making a template

2 Follow the instructions on page 15 for special edging shapes. On your border fabric, draw two straight lines measuring 27in (69cm) and two lines measuring 21in (54cm), with a fabric-marking pencil. Leaving 1¾in (4cm) at the end of each line, carefully draw around your semicircle template until the line is complete. You should have 13 scallops on the longest line and 10 scallops on the shortest. Add a ½in (1cm) seam allowance around the scalloped edge and the base.

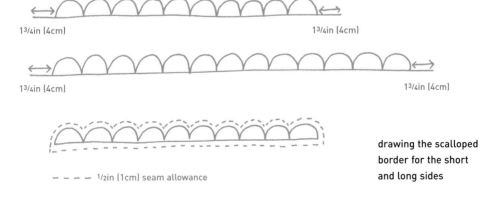

1¾in (4cm)   1¾in (4cm)

1¾in (4cm)   1¾in (4cm)

– – – – ½in (1cm) seam allowance

drawing the scalloped border for the short and long sides

3 Cut out the scallop strips, following the instructions on page 15 to sew the shapes.

Making the pillowcase

4 Cut out two pieces of your chosen fabric for the pillowcase, each measuring 27 x 21in (69 x 54cm). Cut another piece to form the flap of the pillowcase, measuring 5 x 26in (12 x 54cm).

5 If you have access to an overlocker, finish off all the edges of the three pieces of fabric, to prevent fraying. If not, then zigzag stitch the edges by setting your machine to the appropriate stitch settings.

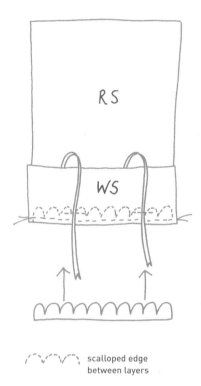

scalloped edge between layers

positioning the flap, scalloped edge, and tape

finishing the edges

6 Place the front section of your pillowcase together with the flap section, right sides together, at one of the shortest sides. Insert a short length of scalloped edging (10 scallops) in between the flap and the pillow-case front. Cut two lengths of tape measuring 10in (25cm) each and insert 5¹/₂in (14cm) in from each edge. When aligning all of the pieces, make sure that all of the raw edges are flush with each other.

7 Set your sewing machine to straight stitch and sew a ¹/₂in (1cm) seam allowance along the edge of the pillowcase and press open.

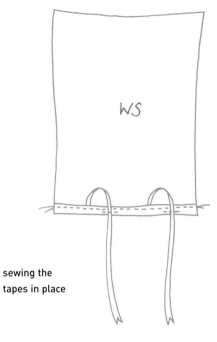

WS

sewing the
tapes in place

8 Take the piece of fabric for the back of the pillowcase and fold over one of the shortest edges by ¹/₂in (1cm) and insert two 10-in (25-cm) lengths of tape into the fold, each 5¹/₂in (14cm) from the side edge. Sew along the folded edge to secure.

9 Fold the ends of the tape outward and stitch down.

10 As before, insert the scalloped edges around the remaining three sides, in between the two layers of fabric, with the two 13-scallop edges down the two longest sides and the remaining short one at the other end. Now place the front section on top of the back section, right sides together, and make sure that the two finished ends are aligned. Secure with pins.

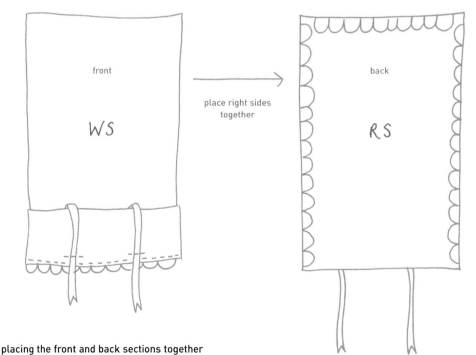

front

WS

place right sides
together

back

RS

placing the front and back sections together

11 Sew the pieces together, paying particular attention when sewing the corners, following the diagram. Cut back the corners and press open the seams. Turn right sides out.

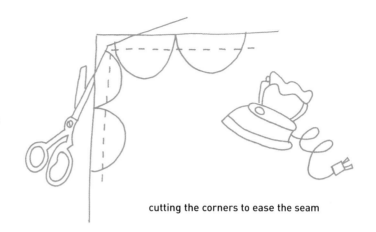

cutting the corners to ease the seam

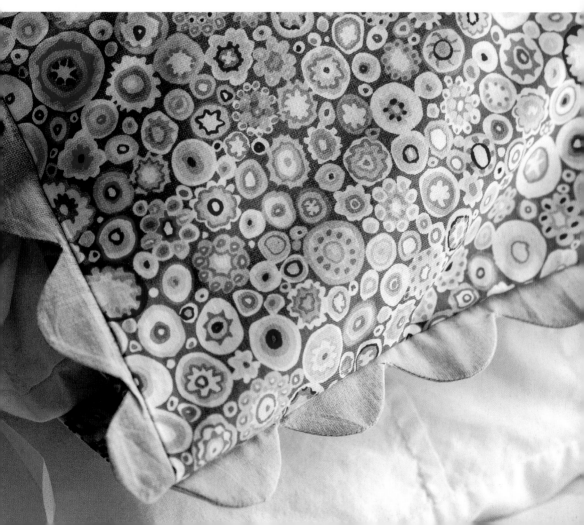

Two-color scarf

★ *This little scarf gains its impact from using two colorways of a fabric pattern, decorated with a few French knots at the ends. Measuring 38½ x 8in (98 x 20cm), it is easy to make if you take care when cutting out the pattern pieces, and very quick to embroider.*

You will need
Pattern paper
½yd (0.5m) each of printed cotton fabric in two colorways
Fabric-marking pencil
Sewing thread to match
Stranded embroidery cotton to contrast
Chenille needle

Making the template
1 Draw a rectangle measuring 40 x 8¾in (100 x 22cm) on pattern paper and cut out the pattern.

2 Fold the paper pattern in half to find the center. Mark this position and following the diagram below carefully, replicate the line shown. Next, cut the pattern piece in half along this line and label one piece A and the other B. You will now have two pattern pieces.

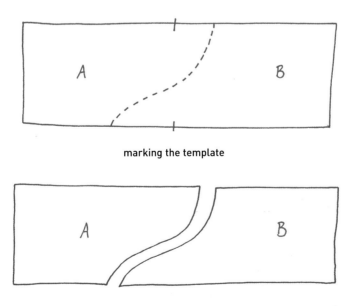

marking the template

cutting the template in half

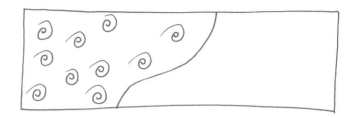

cutting out the pattern pieces
and fitting together

Cutting out the fabric

3 Position the pattern pieces on your fabrics, pin, mark, and cut out on the straight grain. Cut pattern A in both colorways and pattern B in both colorways. Lay the pieces down on a flat surface so that each set of colorways fits together as shown above.

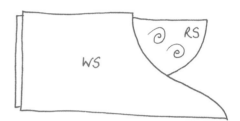

folding one side of scarf with right sides together

4 Fold over each set, right sides together, so the straight short ends align (as shown). Repeat with the other set.

5 Pin the curved edges together, pulling both the sides taut so as to ease the curve lines together.

6 Sew down the curved edge using a ¹/₂in (1cm) seam allowance. To allow for ease, cut into the curve, but do not cut into the stitches. Press the seam open. Repeat with the other two sections.

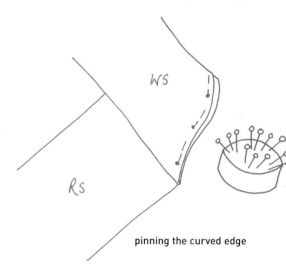

pinning the curved edge

7 Having completed the two panels for the scarf, lay them down on a flat surface and place right sides together. Pin around the edge with a ¹/₂in (1cm) seam allowance.

sewing the sides together,
right sides facing

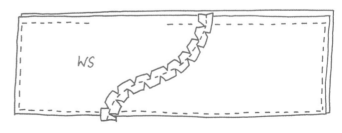

Machine stitch around this edge removing the pins as you go. Leave an opening along the top of about 4in (10cm), cut back the corners and press open the seams.

8 Turn the scarf right sides out and finish off the opening by hand sewing with small stitches. Press and steam again.

9 Embroider French knots randomly over the printed design at the end of the scarf in contrasting stranded embroidery cotton.

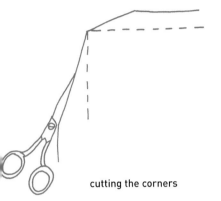

cutting the corners

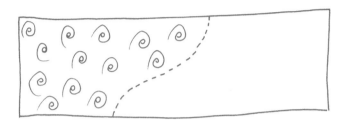

turning the scarf right sides out

Flower necklace and broach

✪✪ *These pretty little folded and stitched flowers can be made individually and sewn onto a cord for a delicate necklace, with a combination of small and large flowers. Alternatively, thread a flower onto a silk ribbon for a bookmark, or follow the variation to make one of the larger flowers as a broach.*

You will need
Scraps of plain cotton fabrics in toning colors
Fabric-marking pencil
Sewing thread to match
Hand-sewing needle
Self-cover buttons: 4 x 1/2in (11mm),
4 x 3/4in (19mm)
Satin cord

Making the flowers
1 Each flower, large or small, needs seven petals. For the smaller flowers, cut out seven fabric squares measuring 11/4in (3.5cm) square; for the larger flowers cut out seven 13/4-in (4-cm) squares.

2 Shaping the petals is a little like origami; for the first stage you need to take one fabric square and fold it in half, wrong sides together, to make a triangle.

3 Next, take the two top corners at each side and fold down so that they meet the bottom tip of the triangle.

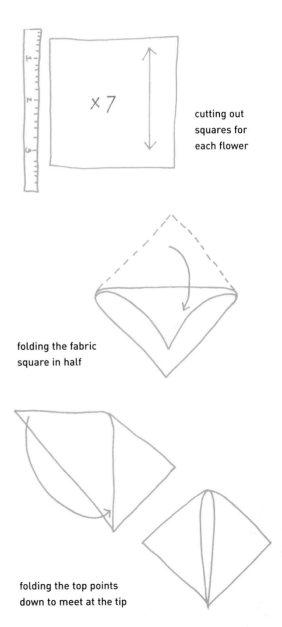

x 7

cutting out squares for each flower

folding the fabric square in half

folding the top points down to meet at the tip

4 Holding the petal carefully, turn the newly formed diamond shape so that the reverse is facing you. Take the two side points and fold to the center back of the diamond.

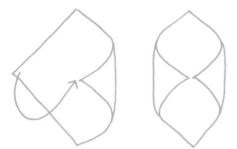

with wrong sides facing, fold the two side points to the center

5 For the final stage, fold the two sides to the middle, so that the two smaller diamond shapes are placed flush against each other. Put a pin through the fabric to hold. Secure in place by sewing a few hand stitches at the back.

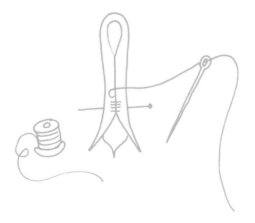

stitching the sides to form a petal

6 Turn the petal to the front and secure with a few hand stitches. Remember to position these stitches near the bottom of the petal as you don't want them to be visible.

adding some stitches to the front

7 Continue to prepare the remaining petals in the same way, making sure that you make enough for the quantity of flowers you require. Join up all the petals by hand sewing a couple of stitches at the base, finishing by joining the last petal to the first. Repeat on the back to ensure that the fabric sits flat.

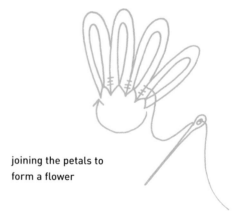

joining the petals to form a flower

Making up the necklace
8 Prepare a self-cover button in matching fabric for each flower you have made (see page 20).

9 Attach the flowers to the button with a matching thread. Line up the loop on the back of the button with the center point where all the petals meet. Secure the button with plenty of stitches to hold it in place.

10 Cut a length of satin cord for the necklace, remembering that it needs to be long enough to fit over your head. Tie a double knot and cut off the excess cord. Position your flowers on the cord and carefully hand stitch them into place.

attaching the flowers to the cord

How to make a flower broach

1 Decide how big you would like the flower on your broach to be, then follow Steps 1–9 above.

2 Having completed your flower, thread a needle with thread that matches the petals of your flower and on the reverse of your flower centralize the broach pin. There are usually three holes on a broach pin, use these holes to secure stitches through the pin and onto the reverse of the flower.

3 To decorate your broach further you could add some stitched leaves. Carefully cut out a leaf shape in felt, then thread a hand-sewing needle with some stranded embroidery cotton and sew running stitches as shown. You can add as many leaves as you like. Finish by hand stitching them to the back of the flower.

joining the petals to
the broach pin

decorating the leaves
with running stitch

stitching the leaves to the back
of the flower

Little tote bag

✪✪✪ *This neat bag can serve many purposes. In the size shown (12½ x 10½in/32 x 27cm), it is a great little handbag, but if made in a larger size it makes an excellent tote. You can decorate it with a couple of simple rows of felt buttons, or make it in a solid-colored fabric and decorate it with a few flowers (see page 58).*

You will need
½yd (0.5m) each of printed cotton (main) and plain cotton fabric (lining)
Iron-on interfacing
Scraps of felt: red and cream
Revolving punch pliers
Stranded embroidery cotton
Chenille needle
Sewing thread to match
Fabric-marking pencil
Loop turner

Cutting out the bag
1 Carefully cut out a rectangle of the main fabric on the straight grain, measuring 13½ x 24½in (34 x 62cm), which includes a seam allowance. Use a set square.

2 Cut out a rectangle to the same measurements in the interfacing. Place the interfacing glue side down on the wrong side of the main fabric. Using an iron, press the fabric and interfacing to bond them together.

Decorating the front
3 At this point, work the hand embroidery that will decorate the bag. The decoration shown was created by punching out circles in

cutting out the bag fabric

pressing the interfacing onto the main fabric

63

felt with revolving punch pliers and attaching them to the bag with French knots (see page 24), but you could use buttons and French knots if you prefer. Position the circles at the short ends of the fabric, an equal distance from each edge.

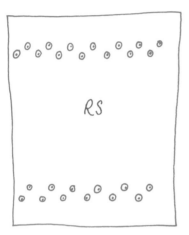

attaching felt circles to the fabric with embroidery

4 Now take the short edge of the bonded rectangle and fold it in half, with right sides together. On your sewing machine set the

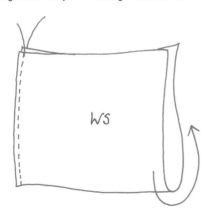

folding the embellished fabric in half and stitching

stitch length to 2.5 and using a ½in (1cm) seam allowance as a guide, stitch down each side of the newly formed square. Press open the seams.

Making the lining
5 Cut out a rectangle from the lining fabric to measure 13½ x 22in (34 x 56cm). Repeat Step 4 to finish the lining.

Making the sides and base
6 To form the base and side panels of your bag, carefully fold flat the bottom corners of the outer fabric into a triangular shape on the wrong side and use the side seams as a guide—these should run down the center. Using a tape measure, measure from the tip of the triangle down each side 1¾in (4cm) and mark this point with a fabric-marking pencil. Making sure the fabric is completely flat, sew across in a straight line from each point marked. Repeat for the lining.

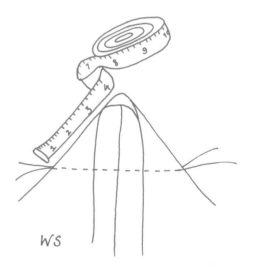

stitching the corners

7 To create the bag base, on the wrong side carefully fold along the front of the bag from the corner stitch lines you have just sewn. Make sure that both folds are parallel, and the fabric is flat. Machine stitch a line almost on the fold of the fabric. Repeat for the other side. This will create a squared-off base.

stitching across the fold

8 Turn the bag right sides out, and fold down 1/2in (1cm) all around the top edge. Press. Then fold under the top edge again 3/4in (2cm) all the way around. Press and pin in place. The bag is now ready for the lining to be inserted.

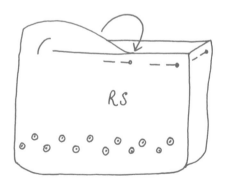

folding in the top of the bag

Finishing the bag

9 Place the lining inside the bag, with wrong sides together. Take care to push the lining into the bottom corners of the bag, and make sure that the side seams align. Tuck the lining up under the fold at the top of the bag. Pin into position.

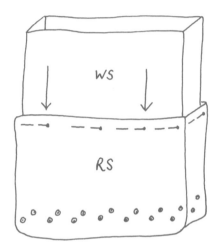

putting the lining inside the bag

10 Prepare the handles for the bag by cutting two pieces measuring 4 x 153/4in (10 x 40cm) in both the main fabric and the interfacing. Iron on the interfacing to the wrong sides. With right sides together, fold over at the longest edge. Sew down the raw edge using a 1/2in (1cm) seam allowance. Using a loop turner, turn the handles to the right side, and press.

sewing the handles

11 From the side seams of your bag, measure in 3in (8cm) along the front and back top of your bag, and mark these positions with a pin. Tuck the handle end ½in (1cm) under the fold on the inside of the bag. Bring the handle up and over the top edge of the bag, and pin and machine stitch across both top and bottom edges of the fold.

12 Repeat Step 11 for the other end of the handle and then repeat the process for the handle on the other side of the bag. Finish off by steaming and pressing the bag.

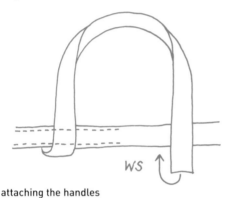

WS

attaching the handles

securing both handles

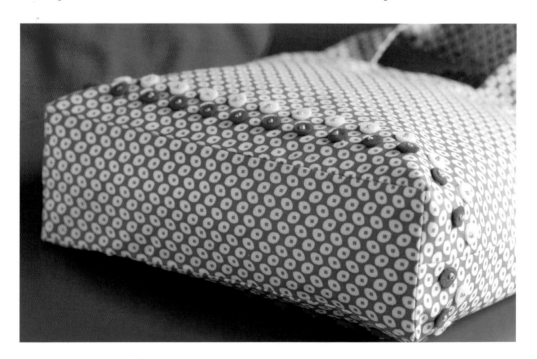

Pom-pom slippers

✪✪ *These cozy slip-ons are surprisingly simple to make. Choose the color of felt to coordinate with your bedroom scheme or robe, or go for a neutral tone, such as the gray used here, so that you can wear them with any outfit for lazy days at home. They can be embellished with embroidery, pom-poms, buttons, appliqué, or a combination of techniques.*

You will need
Pattern paper
Felt: charcoal
Fabric-marking pencil
Leather (or leather insole)
Fabric glue
Tapestry wool yarn in two colors
Chenille needle
Pom-pom maker or piece of card

Preparing the slipper soles
1 Prepare a paper pattern for your slippers. The best way to do this is to draw around your foot or trace around an insole. You will need to enlarge the pattern by 1/2in (1cm) all round. You only need to trace one foot.

2 Cut out four pieces of felt, using the pattern as your guide: two for the left foot, and two for the right. Cut out two pieces of leather using the slipper pattern (or use leather insoles).

3 Sandwich each piece of leather between two pieces of felt. Use fabric glue to secure the three layers together. Repeat the same process for the other slipper.

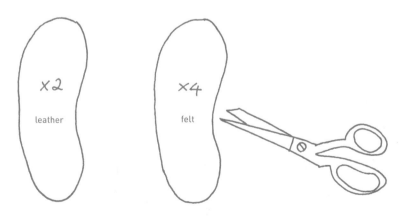

x2
leather

x4
felt

cutting out the felt

Preparing the slipper band

4 Using a tape measure, measure across your foot, from the left side, across the top and back down to the right side at the point where the band will be attached. Add a ¹⁄₂in (1cm) seam allowance to each side and make the band 2¹⁄₄in (6cm) in depth. Make a paper pattern to this measurement and use as a template to cut four pieces in felt.

cutting out the slipper bands

5 Blanket stitch two pieces of felt together along the two longest sides (see page 23) to make the band. Repeat for the other foot.

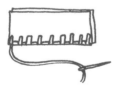

stitching the band with blanket stitch

Constructing the slippers

6 Put your foot on top of the prepared sole and position the band. Place the raw edge of the band to the raw edge of the slipper and pin into place. Blanket stitch around the outside of the sole in a contrasting yarn, making sure that you incorporate the band. Repeat for the other foot.

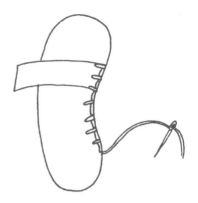

blanket stitching the sole

7 Decorate the top of the band with pompoms made from tapestry wool yarn (see page 27). To finish the pom-pom, dangle it in the steam of a boiling kettle (taking care not to scald yourself): the steam will fluff out the wool. Secure the pom-poms to the tops of the slippers with small hand stitches.

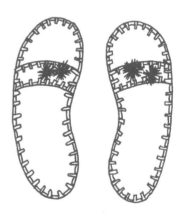

finishing the slippers with pompoms

Embellished borders

✪✪ *To personalize an existing dress or skirt, you can add a contrasting, or matching, border with rouleau loop detail. This will not only look attractive but can be used to lengthen a skirt that is too short. The rouleau edging could also be added to a neckline, by unpicking the existing facing, inserting the rouleau detail, and replacing the facing.*

You will need

Existing dress/skirt
Seam unpicker
Pattern paper
Meter ruler/tape
1/2yd (0.5m) each of contrasting fabrics: one
for the border and one for the rouleau loops
Sewing thread to match
Hand-sewing needle

Making the pattern

1 Unpick the hem of the garment and press
flat. Lay your garment inside out on a large
sheet of paper. Following the two side seams
and using a meter rule, extend the two lines
at the side seams until you reach the new
desired length of the garment.

2 Add a seam allowance of 1/2in (1cm) for
the top (this will extend into the old hem of
your garment) and 3/4in (2cm) for the bottom

hem line of the border. Do this to the front
and back.

3 Make sure that both sides of the border
are exactly the same length. Draw out the
new bottom hemline of the garment by
joining up the two side seams with a gentle
curve. You will need to do the same for the
top of the border, following the curve of the
bottom hemline. Use a ruler to make sure
the border is the same depth all the way
along. Cut out your paper pattern.

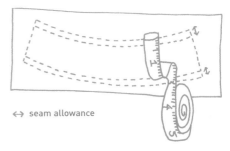

↔ seam allowance

drawing the border

Cutting out the border

4 Fold the paper pattern in half. Take the
fabric you are using for your border and fold
on the straight of grain. Pin the fold of the
pattern to the edge of the folded fabric. Pin
in place and cut out.

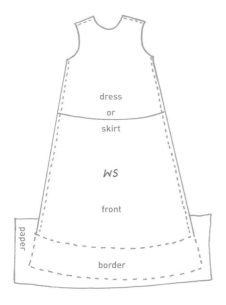

dress
or
skirt

WS

front

border

paper

creating the new border

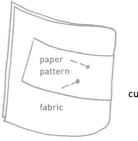

paper
pattern

fabric

cutting out the border

5 Machine around the edge of the border using a zigzag stitch to neaten the edges (it will also prevent them from fraying). With right sides together, sew up the side seams and press open.

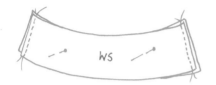

stiching the border side seams

Adding the rouleau loops

6 Make the rouleau tubing from either surplus fabric from your garment or a new contrasting fabric, following the instructions on page 12. Lay and pin the rouleau tubing on the right side of the border fabric around the top edge (raw edge of rouleau to zig-zagged edge). Use the zigzagged edge as your guide. Sew the rouleau loops in place 1/4in (5mm) away from the raw edge.

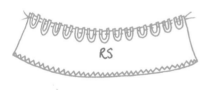

positioning the rouleau loops

Stitching the border

7 Turn the border inside out. With right sides and side seams together, line up the skirt and border zigzagged edges and secure with pins. The border should fit around the bottom of the garment neatly. On the wrong side of the fabric, sew the border and garment bottom together using a 1/2in (1cm) seam allowance.

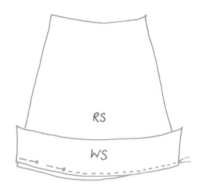

attaching the border

8 Finally, turn up the hem by 3/4in (2cm) and machine stitch in place.

hemming the border

Neckline edging

You could apply a rouleau edging similarly to a neckline. You will need to unpick the existing facing and then sandwich your rouleau tubing between the two layers of fabric, as you did for the contrast hem. Make sure you have made enough rouleau tubing for the purpose (normally three times the length of the area to be embellished). With the garment inside out, baste the tubing in place and pin and resew the facing to the neckline.

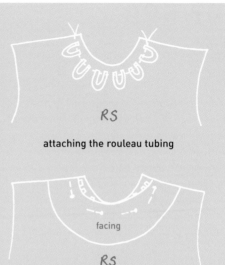

attaching the rouleau tubing

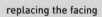

facing

replacing the facing

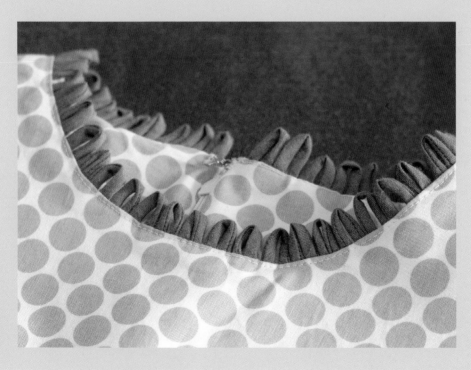

Toy dog

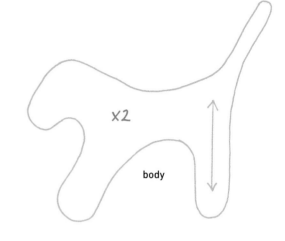

x2

body

⭐ *This little stuffed toy dog is easy to make. It gains much of its charm from the contrast of colors and fabrics used. You can photocopy the pattern pieces to create whatever size you prefer, the one shown here measures 6 x 4¹⁄₂in (15 x 11cm). There is no need to worry about seam allowance. Decide on your choice of main fabric and choose a contrast for the underneath of the toy and insides of the ears.*

You will need

Striped cotton fabric and toning plain cotton fabric
Iron-on interfacing
Fabric-marking pencil
Felt: cream, burnt orange, and charcoal
Stranded embroidery cotton
Chenille needle
Sewing thread to match
Polyester filling or toy stuffing
Fabric glue

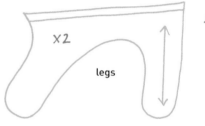

x2

legs

x4

ears

Cutting out the toy dog

1 Iron the interfacing onto the wrong sides of the fabrics (see page 9). Position your pattern pieces on the straight grain of the fabric and carefully trace around the pattern with a fabric-marking pencil. Cut out two body and legs pattern pieces and four ears (two in each colorway).

2 Cut out six patches for the toy in contrasting felt and using stranded cotton, stitch them into place on the main body with a neat running stitch.

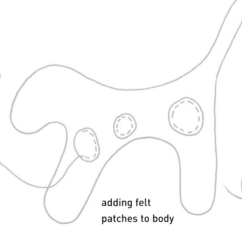

adding felt
patches to body

Stitching the body and legs

3 Taking the two fabric pieces for the underneath section of the body, place right sides together and machine stitch along the straight edge. Press open.

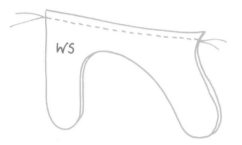

stitching the undersides together

4 With wrong sides together, pin one of the main body sections to the underneath body section, matching up the legs. Repeat for the other piece. At the point where the two fabrics below the tail meet, start to blanket stitch around the edge (see page 23). Keep

checking that the edges meet. Continue until the point at the front where the two fabrics meet. Repeat for the other side of the toy.

Finishing the toy dog

5 Once the legs have been stitched, you can stuff them with the filling, using the eraser end of a pencil. Carefully stuff the four legs, making sure that the stuffing reaches right down to the bottom of each leg.

6 Now join the section of the head up, carrying on from where you finished sewing. At this point take care that all the points join up. Continue around the head, toward the back. As each section is completed, continue to fill with stuffing.

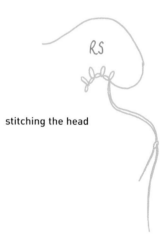

stitching the head

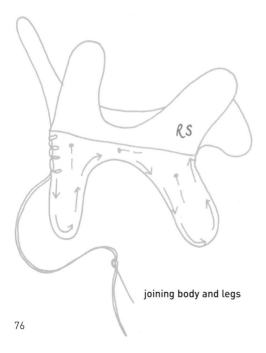

joining body and legs

Finishing the toy dog

7 Once you reach the point at which you started, take care to join all of the fabrics up and finish off your sewing. Then make the ears by blanket stitching around the edge. Repeat for the other ear.

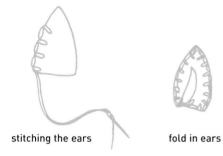

stitching the ears   fold in ears

8 To give the ears a little bit of shape, put a small fold at the base and secure in place with a few hand stitches. Using cotton sewing thread, position on the toy and sew into place.

9 Cut out some eyes and a nose in felt and stick into place.

Animal cushion

✪✪ *This cushion measures 13 x 13in (34 x 34cm), and makes a cute decoration for a child's room. You could make several using different animal faces, following the techniques shown here. Alternatively, use the animal face template as an appliqué for another project.*

You will need

¹/₂yd (0.5m) plain cotton fabric in gold
Coats felt: burnt orange, gold, navy blue, cream, and tan
Fabric-marking pencil
Iron-on adhesive paper
Chenille needle
Tapestry wool yarn in yellow, black, and brown
Sewing thread to match
Pillow form: 13 x 13in (34 x 34cm)

Cutting out the cushion pieces

1 Cut out two pieces of fabric for the front and back of your cushion, one measuring

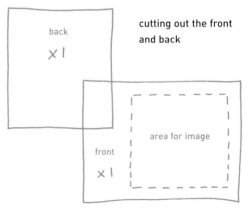

cutting out the front and back

14 x 21¼in (36 x 54cm) for the front, and the other 14 x 10¼in (36 x 26cm) for the back. In order to centralize the design, you will need to place it within the area that measures 12 x 12in (30 x 30cm) on the front of the cushion.

Making the lion face

2 To use the lion design, enlarge the motif templates on pages 90–91. Using the photocopy like a pattern, trace and cut out all of the separate pieces from felt and prepare using iron-on adhesive paper (see page 26). Cut out the outside mane section first. Then cut out the second section of the mane. Cut out the face section.

3 Embellish the details of the lion's face with hand stitches (see pages 22–24) following the diagram below. Use the iron-on

adhesive to bond all of the elements together. When bonding the face you need to work from the back to the front, so start with the outside mane section, then add the inside mane section, bonding this to the outside mane, and finish by putting the face on top, bonding it to the inside mane.

Completing the front and back

4 Use the iron-on adhesive paper to bond the lion's face to the front piece of the cushion, remembering to turn the lion on his side as shown in the diagram below. On the front piece, fold over the right side of the fabric below the lion's face twice by ¾in (2cm) to neaten off the edge; machine stitch to secure. Do the same on one short side of the back section.

ᗰᗰ Tapisserie wool

● French knots

▽ satin stitch

embellishing the face with hand stitches
and bonding the face pieces together

bonding the face to the front of the cushion and
neatening the edges on front and back

Making up the cushion

5 Take the front piece with the lion facing upward and fold over the left-hand edge by 7in (18cm) so that the right sides are on top of each other. Pin to secure. Now take the back piece and, with right sides facing, place the back on top of the front, as shown.

6 Pin a ½in (1cm) seam allowance all the way around the two cushion pieces. Gently curve the two top corners of the cushion.

7 Machine stitch together following the pinned line, removing the pins as you go. Clip into the curves to ease the corners.

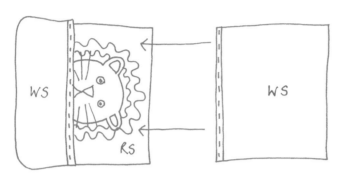

placing the back piece on top of the front with right sides facing

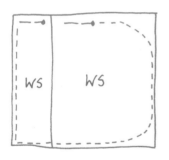

pinning the two pieces and creating a curve

8 Turn the cushion through the opening to the right side. Make a thick braid of 7in (18cm) strands of brown tapestry yarn and tie off in a knot, leaving some loose ends. Sew the tail onto the back of the cushion so that it is visible from the front. Now insert your pillow form.

attaching the tail

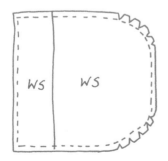

stitching together and easing the corners

Nursery mobile

⭐ *This little mobile is constructed from some dowelling to which are attached a variety of small, colorful felt shapes, such as little animals and birds. It is not difficult to make but, being small, it is a little fussy. Hang it above a baby's crib, making sure it is well out of reach.*

You will need

Felt: lime, cream, tan, gray, gold, orange, baby blue, and burnt orange
Fabric-marking pencil
Stranded embroidery cotton in matching colors
Tapestry wool yarn in various colors
Chenille needle
Polyester filling or toy stuffing
Dowelling: 2 x 10in (25cm) lengths
Cord

Preparing the shapes

1 To make up the shapes for the mobile, use the templates on pages 92–93, or enlarge them to your desired size. Use the photocopy like a pattern and cut out all of the different sections, such as wings, beak, and feet (see page 18). Put the templates on your felt fabric, pin into place, and draw around them. Cut out pairs of shapes as required.

2 As it is easier to hand stitch flat pieces of fabric, embellish the details on each shape separately before you make them up and stuff them. Add the eyes and wings to the front of each piece. Use the hand stitches and the thread guide in the illustrations and key below.

– – – –	running stitch
◍	satin stitch
⟋	Tapisserie wool
╱	Stranded Cotton

embellishing the felt shapes

Assembling the mobile

3 Now begin to put the shapes together. Place them wrong sides together and pin to secure. Stitch around each shape using running stitch, leaving a seam of ½in (1cm). At this point insert the cut-out felt pieces for the duck's feet and the tapestry yarn for the small bird's dangly feet, and sew them in as you go. When making the cat, make the head and body separately. Stop sewing shortly before you reach the point at which you started, you will need this opening to be able to stuff your animal. Sections with no stitches are tucked into the seam and stitched together with the main body.

4 Gently insert a small amount of stuffing into each shape and push it down using the eraser end of a pencil. Continue to fill until the shape is well padded. Use running stitch to close the gap. Join the cat's head and body together.

5 For each animal, cut a long length of cord, varying the lengths from 4¾in (12cm) to 5½in (22cm) and secure it to the top of the padded shape with a few stitches. This will be used to attach the shape to the dowelling.

attaching the hanging cord to the felt shapes

6 Place one piece of dowelling over the other to form a cross. Bind the center using Stranded Cotton. Attach each shape to each of the four ends of the dowelling, knotting the cord over the end.

making a cross from the dowelling

stuffing the felt shapes

7 Take a length of cord approximately 6in (15cm) long and attach it to the center of the crossed dowelling. Use this to hang your mobile from a hook.

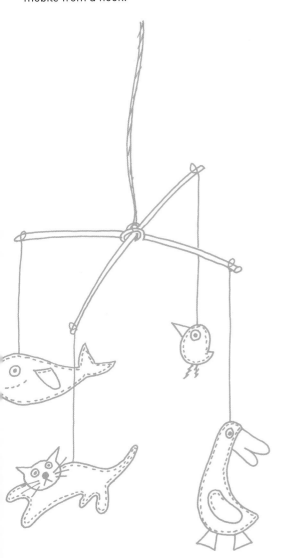

attaching the hanging cord to the dowelling

Appliqué t-shirt

⭐ *This child's t-shirt is simple to make and very unique. You can adapt the idea for a more grown-up version for a teenager, perhaps using a traced image of their favorite pop star, for example.*

You will need
Plain t-shirt
Seam unpicker
Felt: cream, gold, burnt orange
Fabric-marking pencil
Iron-on adhesive paper
Stranded embroidery cotton in bright colors
Chenille needle
Sewing thread to match

Preparing the t-shirt
1 Carefully unpick the two side seams on the t-shirt, using either a seam unpicker or a small sharp pair of scissors. Take care not to cut into the fabric. You are now able to work on the front and the back of the t-shirt.

unpicking the side seams

2 Enlarge the motif on a photocopier or trace to a suitable size for your t-shirt, or draw out your chosen design on paper.

Embellishing the t-shirt

3 Cut out the different pieces of the design from felt and prepare with iron-on adhesive paper (see page 26). Then apply your design to the front of the t-shirt.

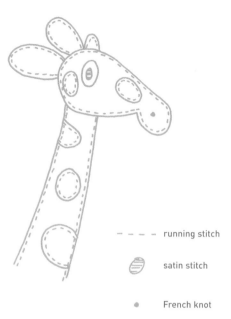

- – – – running stitch

satin stitch

• French knot

embellishing the design

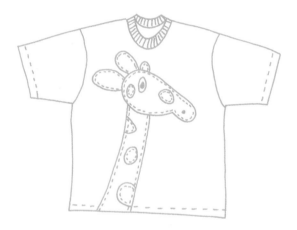

embellishing the t-shirt

4 Next, embellish the design. Here, the design uses running stitch around the giraffe's outline, satin stitch for his eye, and a French knot for his nose (see pages 22–24).

Finishing off

5 When you have finished your appliqué you will need to put the t-shirt back together again. With right sides together, pin the two side seams back in place. Set your sewing machine to a stitch length of approximately 2.5, and carefully sew down the two side seams.

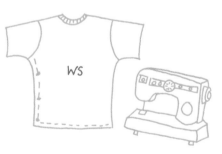

sewing the side seams back together

Alternative motifs

If you wish, you could swap the large motif of the giraffe for a smaller one, such as the duck (right) or indeed any of the other three designs used for the mobile. You will need to enlarge the template of the duck (see page 93) to the size required for a t-shirt.

Then cut out a single piece of each template shape in felt, using felt in tan for the body, gray for the wing, gold for the beak, orange for the feet, and cream for the eye.

Prepare the pieces with iron-on adhesive paper (see page 26) before positioning and pinning them in place to the t-shirt (or other item) as shown below. Iron on to secure.

Embroider around the edges of the shape with a neat running stitch and finish off by embroidering the eye with a French knot (see page 24) in stranded embroidery cotton.

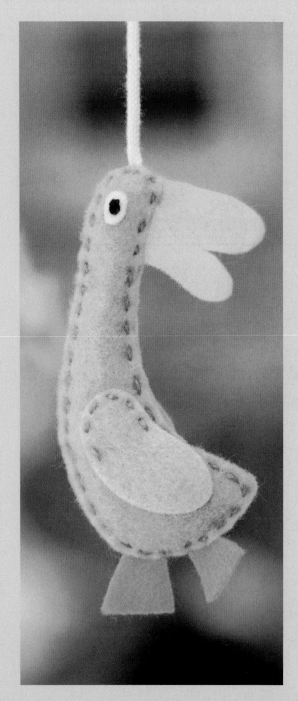

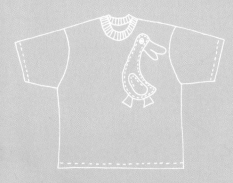

duck motif on t-shirt

Templates

Animal cushion

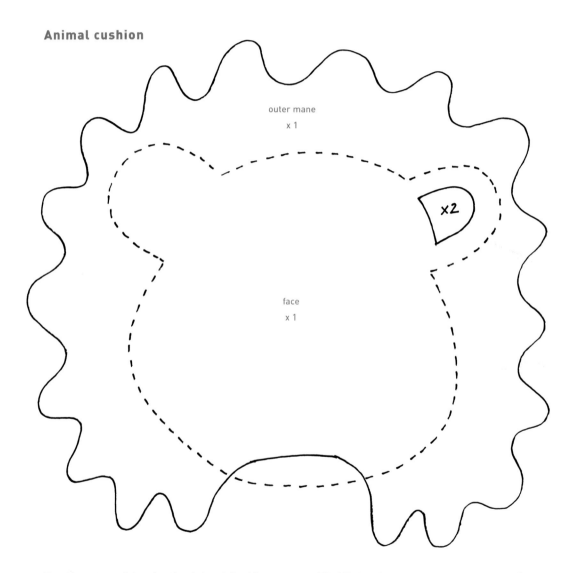

outer mane
x 1

x2

face
x 1

Use these templates for the Animal Cushion on page 78. All the pieces will need to be traced and enlarged to 190 per cent on a photocopier.

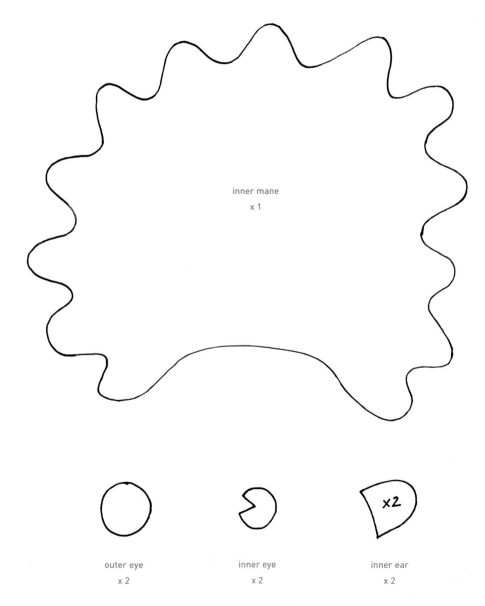

inner mane
x 1

outer eye
x 2

inner eye
x 2

inner ear
x2
x 2

Nursery mobile

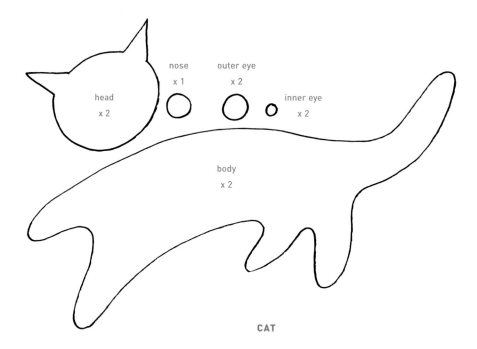

nose
x 1

outer eye
x 2

head
x 2

inner eye
x 2

body
x 2

CAT

Use these templates for
the Nursery Mobile on
page 82. The pieces are
all shown actual size.

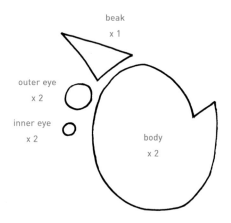

beak
x 1

outer eye
x 2

inner eye
x 2

body
x 2

BIRD

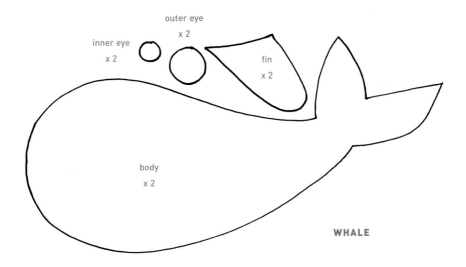

inner eye
x 2

outer eye
x 2

fin
x 2

body
x 2

WHALE

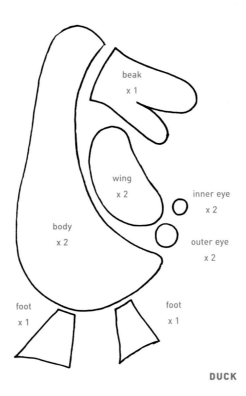

beak
x 1

wing
x 2

inner eye
x 2

body
x 2

outer eye
x 2

foot
x 1

foot
x 1

DUCK

Stockists and suppliers

The fabrics and haberdashery used in this book are all supplied by Coats Crafts UK. The printed cotton fabrics are all supplied by Rowan Yarns (a subsidiary of Coats Crafts UK). Their main addresses are listed below.

More detailed lists of stockists can be found on their websites.

USA

Coats & Clark (Sales Department)
3430 Toringdon Way, Suite 301
Charlotte, NC 28277
tel +001 800 894 3786
www.coatsandclark.com

Westminster Fibers
165 Ledge Street
Nashua, NH 03060
tel +001 800 445 9276
www.westminsterfibers.com

UK

Coats Crafts UK
Lingfield Point
McMullen Road
Darlington, Co. Durham
DL1 1YJ
www.coatscrafts.co.uk
tel +44 (0)1325 394237

Rowan Yarns
Green Lane Mill
Holmfirth
HD9 2DX
www.knitrowan.com
tel +44 (0)1484 681881

ABOUT THE FABRICS

The Rowan cotton fabrics used in this book come in several colorways per design. They are all 100 per cent cotton, in widths of 45in (112cm). The fabric is machine washable at 40 degrees, but remember to allow for some shrinkage, so it is best to wash the fabrics before making up projects.

Coats machine-washable felt has been used for all projects with felt in this book. It is sold in pieces measuring 12in (30cm) square in a wide range of colors.

Index

Acknowledgments

I would like to thank Clare Watson at Coats Crafts UK for giving me the chance to do this book; Susan Berry for her tireless and continuous support throughout; Pauline Smith at Rowan for helping source fabrics; Anne Wilson for the fantastic layouts; John Heseltine for the amazing photographs and Katie Hardwicke for her sharp eye while editing. Also thanks to my family who had to endure the many months of the passionate preoccupation I developed while putting this book together. Thanks, too, to Jayne Emerson for modeling the apron and skirt for the book and Kate Loveday for allowing us to use her house for photography.

Alison Reid